The Sound Of Crickets Chirping In The Backyard

James L. Snyder

Fellowship Ministries
P.O. Box 831313 – Ocala. FL 34483
© 2016 BY FELLOWSHIP MINISTRIES
ALL RIGHTS RESERVED
Unless Otherwise Noted, Scripture
Quotations Are From The Authorized (King James)
Version of The Bible.

ISBN-13:978-1540768636
ISBN-10: 1540768635

WEBSITES
www.whatafellowship.com
www.jamessnyderministries.com

Family of God Fellowship
PO Box 831313 – Ocala, FL 34483
jamessnyder2@att.net
(352) 687-4240

What Readers Say…

Every time you write, "Mistress of the Parsonage," I laugh.

I am a faithful reader of the articles you write in The Troublesome Creek Times in Knott County, KY. I get a smile out of each one. I think you and my husband are "two peas in a pod." Each one sounds like him!! The one about the truck put a smile on my face. He loves his truck!! Keep up the good work, I turn to your articles first.

I enjoy reading your columns in the Riverland News every week, thanks for writing them. There are only a few columnists I read regularly, and of those, I mostly read the subjects that are of particular interest or importance to me. Your writing is something I look forward to each week just for simple pleasure. Your wit is peppered with wisdom that often brings a smile to my face.

Thanks for expressing many of the things I've been thinking, but couldn't articulate!

Each week I read your column in the Buffalo Criterion, and enjoy your take on life wrapped in a scriptural message. After laughing to tears, I decided to reach out to let you know how much I enjoy your column.

Yeah! a great column with the segue into the gospel! wonderful! Appreciated the clarity also, as so many think you have to do something, or continue to be good, etc. to maintain your heavenly gift. I am amazed at how few have ever been told the gospel, seems we are too shy, embarrassed, afraid, who knows. Just keep it up, pastor. Great job.

I have enjoyed your column for some time now and thought it would be nice to email you and let you know. I thoroughly enjoy your sense of humor as you have given me many laughs. I also enjoy you skill in tying in a scripture with your message. The one word that comes to mind when you do this is: smooth.

Our local newspaper, The Salem Leader, is a twice-a-week paper. Your column makes me wish it was once a week. HaHa Just kidding!!! Actually, I am wishing for many more of your columns in the future. Please continue to share your gifts as one hillbilly here in Southern Indiana reads your column before any other part of the paper. Best wishes,

Table of Contents

1. There Is No Known Cure For Happy-itis 7
2. It Was Lights Out At The Old Parsonage 11
3. Acting A Fool Is A Full-time Occupation 15
4. Are Cows Really Holy? 19
5. I Don't Get Headaches, ... 23
6. I Lost My Mind But I Really Haven't Missed It 27
7. My Amazing Fascination With Summer 31
8. Is Confession Really Good For The Soul? 35
9. Not Smart Enough To Be An Idiot 39
10. Apple Fritter: The Fruit Of My Choice 43
11. The Squirrel And Birds Controversy 47
12. How Many Mondays Are There In One Week? 51
13. Pinching Pennies In A Nickel Economy 55
14. Thoughts, Plots And Other Dangerous Activities ... 59
15. Bad Breath Ain't Always That Bad 63
16. Where Have All The Clowns Gone? 67
17. How Did The Devil Get My Cell Phone Number? .. 71
18. Apart From That, I'm Doing Fine! 75
19. The Sound Of Crickets Chirping 79
20. The Only Contest I Really Win Each Year 83

Chapter 1
There Is No Known Cure For Happy-itis

Now that the pressure of the Old Year is off and the New Year has just begun, I can chill out a little and rest for a while.

Towards the end of the Old Year, there is a lot of pressure to get caught up on all of those stupid New Year's resolutions I made for the year. Every year I am pressured into making some silly New Year's resolution. I would think that after a while this would get old.

For some people, this is simply a way of life and addressing the New Year.

"Have you got your New Year's resolution list made up," my wife always badgers me.

I used to be able to get away with saying, "Yes, I sure do."

That worked until one year she said, "Can I see your list of New Year's resolutions?"

I dodged that for as long as I could and then had to confess that I really did not have any New Year's resolutions.

That was a major mistake on my part because the Gracious Mistress of the Parsonage volunteered to help me make up a list of New Year's resolutions. That list was so long that, if taken seriously, it would take me the rest of my life just to put a little dent in it.

From then on, I made up my own little list of New Year's resolutions.

Usually on my list is one resolution dealing with losing weight. I cannot tell you how many times I have lost a pound only to find it and its friend the next day. I cannot help it, I guess I am so pleasant to be around this weight cannot stay away from me. Maybe I should try to be a little grumpier this year. (That would make a great New Year's resolution!)

Somebody in our house is very serious about New Year's resolutions.

The year starts out with, "You got your New Year's resolutions all ready?"

It then evolves into, "Have you started on your New Year's resolutions yet?"

The next evolutionary point is, "What New Year's resolution have you completed?"

The evolution ends with, "Have you completed your New Year's resolutions yet?"

This is one reason why I do not believe in the theory of evolution.

At each evolutionary stage, my stress level increases appropriately. By the time December comes around my life has evolved to a point of absolute nervous recklessness and major stress because I know not one of those New Year's resolutions were met.

That is why I like January. Yes, I have that list of New Year's resolutions, but I have not really started thinking about them yet. That is the beauty of January. Nobody is thinking about working on those resolutions nor is anybody, especially in my happy domicile, questioning about where we are along with our New Year's resolutions.

For the most part, January finds me in a state of sheer happiness. I call it, happy-itis and as far as I know, there is absolutely no cure for it. I just love being happy and on occasion my face joins in the celebration.

"Why," my wife demands, "are you so happy?"

This is where a husband has to carefully think about his next response. Should I tell her the truth or should I tell her what she really wants to hear? Sometimes these two do not hold hands.

I compromise and say, "I'm just happy about starting a new year and what it has for us." Then I smile broadly, which usually throws her off her game.

Being happy is one of the great benefits of life that not many people have discovered. I know there are many times when happiness does not really fit the occasion, but I am concentrating on those times when it does fit. I love being happy.

Not only that, but I love trying to make other people happy as well. Wherever you go these days all you find are people under stress and discouraged without much motivation to go forward. I think everybody needs a dose of happiness every now and again.

I am hoping that somehow I could be infected with the happy-itis virus and infect as many people as I can. Of course, I know there is absolutely no cure for this disease and if I ever find anybody looking for a cure, I am going to go after them with everything I got. (That would make a great New Year's resolution!)

Often when facing a serious problem, my wife will look at me and say, "Wipe that smile off your face right now. Let's get serious for a change."

That has been my problem. It is very difficult, especially during the month of January, for me to get serious about anything. Everything I see brings a smile to my face. Every person I meet causes me to giggle and when I giggle, it is hard to hide it from my face.

James understood this when he wrote, "Behold, we count them happy which endure. Ye have heard of the patience of Job, and have seen the end of the Lord; that the Lord is very pitiful, and of tender mercy" (James 5:11).

There is more to life than being happy, but not much more. Happiness comes from deep inside and flows to the outside so everybody can see it and benefit from it.

Chapter 2
It Was Lights Out At The Old Parsonage

As long as I can remember, at my age that does not go back very far, I have always been an early riser. I do not like to stay in bed any longer than I have to. So much I want to do and so little time I need an early start every day.

I have always used Benjamin Franklin's motto for myself, "Early to bed and early to rise makes one healthy, wealthy and wise." Unfortunately, my early to bed and early to rise may have made me healthy, but certainly not wealthy or wise.

This past week an event happened that challenged my "early to rise" regimen.

As usual, I rose early and headed for the kitchen for my cup of coffee. There is no way I can start a day without first indulging in my early morning cup of Joe. Nothing starts the day off better than a hot cup of coffee.

I am not sure who invented coffee, but I sure would like to buy them a cup of coffee and shake their hand. People, who do not really know any better, complain that coffee is bad for your health. Believe me when I say the absence of my coffee is bad for everybody's health around me.

I go to bed early dreaming of that first cup of coffee when I rise.

Stumbling to the kitchen, I stubbed my toe twice walking down the hallway and then tried to turn on the kitchen lights. I am very careful to be quiet so as to not awaken the other resident in the house. She is the sort of person that needs her rest. I am the kind of person that wants her to have all the rest she can get. Therefore, I try to quietly go to the kitchen and turn on the coffee pot.

When I flipped the light switch, nothing happened. I mumbled to myself that the light bulb probably burnt out. Have you ever noticed that that happens when you need the light the most? How many times does a light bulb go out during the day?

I tried several light switches in the kitchen and the dining room and none worked. "Well," I thought to myself, "I will start the coffee." I fumbled my way to where the coffee pot was and turned the switch on. Nothing happened.

I then went to turn on the TV to catch some early news and nothing happened.

There was no electricity at all in the house. My challenge was to make sure the electricity works before my wife got up. I could not let her know that we had no electricity.

Nothing I did restored any kind of electricity in our house.

Then it happened.

My wife came stumbling down the hallway and the first thing out of her mouth was, "Turn the lights on."

I explained to her that there was no electricity and nothing was working in the house.

The next thing out of her mouth was, "Did you pay the electric bill?"

That did occur to me and there was a good probability that I had not paid the electric bill.

Fortunately, I had my cell phone and was able to call the electric company only to find out that the electricity in our neighborhood was out and the restoration in our neighborhood was estimated to be at around 10 o'clock.

How in the world can I survive without my cup of coffee until 10 o'clock in the morning? The whole world is in danger!

I never realized how important electricity was. I just took it for granted, paid the bill every month and just enjoyed the appliances and the lights and most important of all, the coffee pot.

As much as I love my coffee pot, it does not work without the electricity. I had a few words with the coffee pot, but it did not do any good. It wanted electricity and would not work until it had electricity. How legalistic!

Standing around in the darkness of the early morning my wife and I stared at each other, at least I think we were staring at each other, and wondering what in the world we could do. I was so afraid she would come up with a solution. She always does, you know. No matter what I break, she can fix. Now we had this problem before us.

Then she said those terrible anticipated words, "Why don't we go out for breakfast this morning?"

Being married as long as I have been, I realized this was not a question requiring an answer, but rather it was something she wanted us to do. And so, off to the restaurant we went for our early morning coffee.

What I want to know is, will the electric company reimburse me for my early morning breakfast? After all, it is their fault that we had to go out. If I ever miss paying my bill, they always charge me late fees. Turnabout, I believe, is fair play.

I appreciate what David said, "For the LORD God *is* a sun and shield: the LORD will give grace and glory: no good *thing* will he withhold from them that walk uprightly" (Psalms 84:11).

Many times, we never miss something until it is no longer available. I do not want that to happen to me concerning God's grace and mercy in my life.

Chapter 3
Acting A Fool Is A Full-time Occupation

My paternal grandfather's favorite holiday was April 1. He would spend months putting together some trick to fool either a family member or a friend. Both were assessable to his "tricks."

He could read a person and within a few moments have an idea of what the best trick to play on that person. Nobody really saw it coming. They knew his reputation, of course, but he was so skillful in his acts of foolery that nobody ever guessed they were a target until it was too late.

One thing I learned from my grandfather is that it is almost impossible to fool the Fool-Master. If he had spent as much time being a grandfather as being a reputable Fool-Master, he would have been the greatest grandfather in the world. His priorities, however, were not in that direction.

One thing my grandfather never did was reveal how he could pull off these tricks on people. At times he came close but that was his secret he took to his grave.

Those who tried to pull a trick on him usually have it backfire and turned out to be a Major-Fool. I know my cousins and I spent hours trying to figure out a foolproof plan to pull on our grandfather. The problem was, he died before we could finally put together anything that would come close.

Thinking about that recently, I was pondering the idea that it really takes a lot of time to be a fool. In fact, some people make it a full-time job.

With my grandfather, acting a fool was just a hobby. He could turn it on and he could turn it off and got a lot of fun out of pulling tricks on people who were not expecting such a trick from such a man. Other people carry this kind of foolery into every aspect of their life without even trying. They just simply are fools in everything they do. Now, I am not sure, does this comes naturally or do they have to work at it.

There are times when a person needs to be serious and then there are times when a little dab of foolery will do. To be serious all the time can lead, according to my grandfather, to a serious nervous breakdown. Who in the world wants that!

I must confess I am not my grandfather, although there have been times in which I yearned to be. His great accomplishment in life was to make fools out of people who thought they were smart and uppity.

I wish I knew how to do that!

I, on the other hand, need to work very hard at not being a fool. Believe me, it is a full-time job. It is so easy to be a fool. At least from my perspective.

I cannot tell you how many times the Gracious Mistress of the Parsonage has looked at me and said rather sternly, "Are you acting like a fool?"

Although we have been married for years, she has not really concluded that I cannot act. I am what I am, I am what you see, no thespian arts about it. I wish I was acting a fool, because then I could stop acting and become a normal person, whatever that is.

When I feel down on myself in this area, I think of many of the fools in the world around us. And we all know who we are.

I think the biggest fools in my book are those who are afraid of words. Words seem to upset and unnerve causing them to go into some kind of psychotic spin. I do not understand because a word is simply a word.

There are three letters in the English alphabet that brings more agitation and hatred than any other letters. Just three words.

The three letters are D O G. Of course, when you see those letters you immediately think of one of your favorite little animals. A dog is a friendly kind of a thing. When somebody sees these three letters, they usually smile. However, they are just three letters in the English alphabet. Nothing more than that.

Organize these letters and many people will go bizarre. For example, if we arrange the letters G O D, people will go crazy. They are afraid of these three letters so arranged.

These same letters make up the word dog. Yet if you reverse those letters and make it spell God, people get all agitated and upset and want to put a band on those letters.

Usually, the ones who are the most upset about these three letters so arranged are some of the highly educated people in our country. I simply do not get it. If they are so educated and sophisticated, why do three letters in the English alphabet frighten them?

I find it a little strange that the people who do not believe in God, are the ones most agitated by the letters G O D. If they do not believe in God, what are they afraid of? If, in their sophisticated opinion, God does not exist, then why are they afraid of three letters in the English alphabet?

David put this in the proper perspective. "The fool hath said in his heart, *There is* no God. They are corrupt, they have done abominable works, *there is* none that doeth good" (Psalms 14:1).

Happy holiday to those who qualify.

Chapter 4
Are Cows Really Holy?

As an amateur wordsmith, I am fascinated with words and phrases. I love my cell phone because I have a dictionary and thesaurus all ready for my personal touch and I can research any word or phrase I hear.

You can tell a lot about a person by the words and phrases they use. Of course, most use words and phrases they have no idea what they mean. Perhaps they heard somebody else say these words or phrases and so they incorporate them into their vocabulary, which, says more about them than anything else.

I grew up in a very strict Amish/Mennonite community where speech was a very guarded activity. Although not Amish or Mennonite, I still had to be careful what I said and how I said it. Curse words were completely off limit. No circumstance ever existed, according to these people, warranting any curse word.

My maternal grandfather was like this. He never had much to say and did not say that very often. I remember one time sitting on the front porch with my grandfather and his brother and we spent the whole afternoon together and probably did not say five words between the three of us. My grandfather certainly was not outspoken in anything.

Whenever he got angry with my grandmother, he simply would leave the house, walk down to the barn and who knows what he did venting his anger at the time.

Venting anger is quite an occupation these days. Whether a religious venue, a political venue or just some educational venue, people are filled with anger and are trying to vent it somehow and from what I see much of it is not working.

An old saying goes, "Sticks and stones may break my bones but names will never hurt me." Yet, names do really hurt us.

One phrase my grandfather used a lot was, "holy cow." He was a farmer so I instinctively thought he was talking about his cows. Why his cows were holy and others were not was something I could never comprehend. But, he was my grandfather.

I still remember the first time I heard him say that phrase; "Holy cow, it's hot outside today."

When he said it, I was rather confused. What does a cow have to do with it being hot outside and are cows really holy? It just did not make any sense to me.

Another favorite phrase was, "Holy cow, I'm tired."

Again, what does a cow have to do with him being tired? Maybe he worked a lot with the cows. I know he had about a half a dozen dairy cows and he milked them all by hand. Maybe that is what he was talking about.

But the thing that really got me was what in the world does "holy" have to do with a cow?

As I got older, I began to realize that "holy" and "cow" had nothing to do with each other. It was just a phrase my grandfather used, and, to put it mildly, it really meant nothing at all.

As I get older, the more I realize that people say things they really do not mean. In fact, most people do not really think about what they are saying let alone know what they are saying.

As an amateur wordsmith myself, I like to parse my words very carefully. I want to know what I am saying and say what I am thinking. Of course, according to the Gracious Mistress of the Parsonage, thinking is not at the top of my list of activities. I cannot disagree with her on that one.

Yes, words do matter. I need to be careful what I am saying, the more important it is, the more I need to be careful to understand what the other person is hearing. One of the things I have learned as a husband is that what I am saying to my wife may not be what my wife is hearing.

Yes, sticks and stones can break my bones, but that is nothing to what harm words can do.

At a real desperate point in my life, I responded to an incident involving my wife and almost automatically, the phrase, "Holy Cow," came tumbling out of my mouth. Needless to say, it was the last time anything like that ever happened.

My wife looked at me with one of "those looks," and said, "Holy what?"

How can you explain something you do not understand yourself? She looked at me, I look back at her with one of those blank stares I am famous for, and had no idea what she was talking about.

She had no idea what I was talking about and so I thought at least we were even. But not so.

I had to promise her "and cross my heart and hope to die," never to use such a phrase again. "That phrase," she said most defiantly, "is not permitted in this house." She said it in such a way that I have, to this very day, never questioned her on it and have never used that phrase again.

James warned about this when he wrote, "Even so the tongue is a little member, and boasteth great things. Behold, how great a matter a little fire kindleth!" (James 3:5).

I do not know if cows are holy or not, but I will never put those two words together in a phrase whatsoever as long as the sun shines.

Chapter 5
I Don't Get Headaches, I Give Them

This past week I got myself into some rather unnecessary trouble. I say unnecessary because it was trouble that I could have avoided if I only would have thought before I spoke.

This is one of the greatest crosses that I bear in my married life. I always speak before I think because I do not have that much time to speak. If you know what I mean.

The Gracious Mistress of the Parsonage was complaining that she had a headache and did not know how to get rid of it. At first I thought she was referring to the other person who lived in the parsonage with her, but I soon discovered she had a headache and it seemed to be very painful.

As a husband, one of my duties is to try to make my "helpmeet" as comfortable as possible. Although I have been married a lifetime, I still have not acquired much expertise on wifeology.

She was complaining about this headache and so I thought I would step in or step up, whichever the case, and tell her, "Don't worry about your headache. It's all in your head." At the time I did not know what I was saying.

When I did say it, she glared at me with one of "those" glares. Every husband knows exactly what I am talking about.

The thing that hurt the most was she did not say anything, she just glared.

This just shows the compatibility of our household. Every household, every relationship needs glue to hold it together. This is our glue. She gets headaches and I give them.

I am not sure I have had more than a half a dozen headaches in my entire life. But I can assure you, I have given plenty a headache to a variety of people. That's my specialty. Some doctors have a remedy for headaches and others, like me, know how to give them right smartly.

I suppose the reason I do not get very many headaches is because there is nothing up there to ache. If I would clutter my head with all sorts of things I would run the danger and possibility of acquiring a headache.

One of my specialties is that I can think for a long period of time about nothing. I can stare into space and not be thinking about anything whatsoever.

Usually, at one of these empty staring times the wife will ask, "What are you thinking about?"

Perhaps that is what a headache really is. Being asked something you have no idea how to answer. How do you tell someone that you are not thinking about anything when it looks like you are thinking about something? And, what is the difference between "anything" and "something?"

Oh boy. I think I'm getting a headache right now.

When my wife gets a headache she takes medication, lays down on the couch, puts a heating pad around her neck and before she closes her eyes she looks at me as though daring me to make a noise.

Do not let this out, but sometimes her headache gives me a headache.

Really, the only thing that gives me a headache are things inconveniencing me at the time.

Like two weeks ago I had to take a two hour trip on I-75. Now, the speed limit is 70 mph. Normally I can handle that, I just said my speed control thingamajig and go cruising (or is it trumping?) down the highway.

The headache came when there was an accident which brought the traffic to an amazing 2 mph. I do not mind stopping, but when it is moving 2 mph, it is really a headache.

Then, coming north on the same highway there was another accident, but this time we were going 3 mph.

Talk about a headache.

I know what you are thinking. You are thinking that my headache is not nearly as bad as my wife's headache. All I can say is, how do you know?

One person's headache is very real to them, as real as another person's headache is to them.

The problem with my headache on the highway was, I could not take any medication, lie down and put a heating pad on my neck and go to sleep. I had to stay awake and watch where in the world I was going even though I was not going very fast.

Gladly would I have traded my headache on the highway for her headache on the couch.

Of course, there is always the idea that I cause headaches. And I suppose there's not much I can do about that. Except, maybe, try not to cause a headache. But when you're person like me, you don't know you're causing a headache until you've caused that headache.

What would life be without headaches either getting them or giving them? I suppose that's what life is all about. If you think you can live your life without getting or giving a headache you are in for a truly severe migraine.

As I thought about this I was reminded of a very special verse of Scripture. "And God shall wipe away all tears from their eyes; and there shall be no more death, neither sorrow, nor crying, neither shall there be any more pain: for the former things are passed away" (Revelation 21:4).

In this life you can't get away from headaches, but I have something to look forward to and that is what God has for me.

Chapter 6
I Lost My Mind But I Really Haven't Missed It

I am notorious for losing things. I do not know what it is about me, but I cannot keep track of anything I own. If you want to lose something and never find it again, simply put it into my trust. I am the king of losing things. My problem is, I do not lose the right things.

Why I am so klutzy in this area is beyond my ability to comprehend. Some of my most treasured items have been lost for all time. Even the other day I lost a lot of time searching for something I could not find. That is the reason I try not to become attached to anything I own.

The Gracious Mistress of the Parsonage has become frustrated many times because of something she gave me and it is now no longer to be found anywhere this side of the blue moon. She has given me lecture after lecture along this line dealing with personal responsibility and as always, I take personal responsibility for losing everything that I have.

What more can I possibly say?

A few things that I have lost I kinda wished I had back. I remember a pocket knife I was quite attached to and had it for quite a while until one day there was nowhere to be found. Believe me, I looked everywhere. Of course, I could not have looked everywhere or I probably would have found it. Why is it that when you lose something you usually find it in the last place you look?

The one question that I ponder more than anything else is, where do things go when they are lost? Is there a particular place where lost things gather and have a party until someone finds them? If there is I would like to know where that place is. Of course, with my luck, that place is lost.

Everything I have lost throughout life I have gotten over. The aforementioned pocket knife, I have replaced at least 27 times. It would be great one day to find all 27 of those lost knives? Then I would march my way to eBay!

I have gotten over just about everything that I have lost and adjusted my life to not having that particular thing. There is one thing, however, that I still have not gotten over.

I am not exactly sure when I lost it, because I did not really use it that much. Oh, once in a while I might have used it, but not very regularly.

The thing I am referring to is my mind. I cannot find out or remember the exact date when I lost my mind. I am not sure where I was when I lost it. Maybe if I knew where I was at when I lost my mind, I could go back and search a little bit and maybe find it.

I know that I had a mind up until I got married. I do remember using my mind up until that point. The thing is, I do not know what happened to my mind after I got married. Where did it go?

Of course the thought is probable that I still have my mind, but I am not using it. It would make sense in a certain regard. But what is my mind doing while I am not using it? Is somebody else using my mind?

For instance. Some people will ask me about something and I usually respond, "Okay, I really don't mind if you do that."

Or, "That's quite all right. I don't mind at all."

Of course that has its limit. Someone walked up to me on the street the other day and ask if they could borrow five dollars from me. Then, I did mind. Where my mind came from at that point I will never know, but I am certainly glad it arrived on time.

That brought me to the place of thinking that maybe I have not lost my mind. Maybe my mind is hiding somewhere and only appears in emergencies. If that is the case, I really don't mind.

I remember the old saying that goes something like, "mind over matter, and if you don't mind it don't matter."

Just the other day my wife said, "Do you mind if we go out for supper tonight?"

Now I was in a dilemma. Where is my mind when I really need it?

I did mind, but I could not find my mind and so all I could say was, "I don't mind if that is what you want to do."

Where in the world did that come from? I did mind, but my mind was not available to bail me out of an activity closely linked to my wallet.

I think my mind is hiding somewhere and waiting to have a little bit of fun with me. However, I really don't mind because if I did mind, I would be in so much trouble and my real mind would be so confused that it probably would never mind again.

Actually, I have not really missed my mind.

The apostle Paul had a different twist to this. He said," Let this mind be in you, which was also in Christ Jesus" (Philippians 2:5).

I may have lost my mind, but my real focus in life is to lose myself in the mind of Christ.

Chapter 7
My Amazing Fascination With Summer

It comes as a great relief to me that winter is over and summer has stepped up and taken its rightful place. I really love summer. I am fascinated with all aspects associated with summer.

Some people, like the Gracious Mistress of the Parsonage, enjoy the aspects of winter, primarily the cold. I just do not like the cold. I will accept a cold shoulder occasionally, but that is as far as I will go in the area cold.

Winter has no aspects of fascination for me. I do not like being cold, shivering and my nose tingling with frostbite. Winter is certainly not for me.

During the wintertime, I have to wear all kinds of clothing and coats and sweaters. In the summer time, I can relax, sit on the back porch with a glass of iced tea and enjoy the butterflies floating through the flowers. Ah, what a wonderful time summer is.

This brings up the sharp difference between my wife and me. For some reason she loves winter. This may have something to do with her growing up in upper state New York where it is snowy and wintry all the time. I remember visiting once in August and just about froze to death.

But she enjoys chilly temperatures. She enjoys when the temperature falls below 70.

I have a basic rule in life. When the temperature falls below my age, I'm cold. Each year it seems to be getting a little higher.

The thing about summer is simply this; when it gets really, really hot, I simply turn on the air conditioner, which truly works. Not so much in the winter. No matter how cold it is I cannot seem to get the temperature high enough to ward off that chilly, frosty feeling.

I know in the middle of winter we have a holiday called "Christmas." Have you ever noticed how Santa Claus dresses?

He is extremely overweight, all that insulation under his skin, plus he wears a huge red coat with a hat. Most of the time he is also wearing gloves. If he really enjoyed winter, he would experience winter in the beauty of its rawness.

However, summer for me has many amenities. For example, you can tell your wife that you are going fishing and never actually get to the lake to do any fishing. Along the way, you see a nice area where people are having picnics and just sitting under some lovely trees. Basking in the sunlight of summer is worth all that it is made up to be.

Summer is also the time for picnics.

It begins with Memorial Day, which is the first picnic day of the summer. From then on there is a picnic day set for every month of the summer. In fact, in July, I make sure there are two picnic days just in case I miss the first one.

The beautiful thing about a picnic is you can eat with your fingers. In the house, the wife wants me to eat with forks and spoons and all of that kitchenware stuff. Out on the picnic table I can eat as I am supposed to eat: with my fingers.

Summer is the time to chill out. During the winter you are running here and there and trying to catch up with this holiday and that holiday. Summer is the time to slow down and enjoy the sunshine.

I am not sure why there are more holidays throughout the winter than there are during the summer, but I sure am grateful for the person who set up that calendar. Summer is not celebrating this holiday and that holiday; summer is enjoying the outdoors as much as possible.

Just the other day I was heading out the door and the wife called after me and said, "Where are you going?"

I thought about that for a moment, smiled and said, "I don't know where I'm going."

There was a slight pause and then she said, "Can I go with you?"

The beautiful thing about summer is that you can go somewhere without going anywhere. Nothing is more pleasant than having nowhere to go and taking your time getting there.

If I had anything to do with it, and I certainly don't, I would make sure there would be summer the year round. I will never, ever get tired of the summer time.

Sitting on the porch one afternoon the wife came out and said, "What are you doing? Don't you have something to do?"

I rocked back and forth three times without even looking at her and said, "I'm doing nothing and liking every moment of it."

She then joined me in doing nothing and we did nothing for the rest of the afternoon. I had things to do. She, of course, had things to do. But we just joined our hearts in doing nothing together. Nothing is better than a summer afternoon when you can do nothing together and enjoy every moment of it.

I like with the preacher said, "I said in mine heart, God shall judge the righteous and the wicked: for *there is* a time there for every purpose and for every work" (Ecclesiastes 3:17).

If there is a time for work, then there should be plenty of time for rest. If I don't get my rest, how can I do the work that I have to do?

Chapter 8
Is Confession Really Good For The Soul?

I have a confession to make. My first confession, of course, is that I do not always make confessions. Not that I don't have things to confess, but I am rather slow in owning up to what I am doing and confessing it.

For example. When the Gracious Mistress of the Parsonage says, "Who forgot to put the milk back into the refrigerator?" I usually pretend I did not hear her and try avoiding any kind of confession.

After all, why should I confess to something that she knows is true already? I am not sure why she asked such questions; I only can think that she is trying to rub it in or something. I do confess that I do not confess as often as I should.

Not that I don't believe in confessing. I talk about it all the time but when it comes to me, I can always come up with a reasonable explanation of what I did or did not do. My philosophy is simply this; if you can explain your action why confess doing it?

And so, I need to clear my soul and make a good confession.

My wife and I agree on one level. Both of us leaned towards being workaholics. She leans further than I do, I will confess. But I also suffer problems in the workaholic area.

This is one reason why I do not really appreciate holidays for what they really are. Taking a day off does not seem like a very good thing to do, from my perspective. I do not mind working 24/7.

Isn't this the reason God gave us laptop computers? No matter where I go, I can take my work with me. Hallelujah, and pass me another job to do.

On our vacation, the wife spends all her time checking out the thrift stores in the area. Believe me, that is a job in itself. I, on the other side of the vacation, usually stay in the room making conversation with my computer. There is always another article to do, another sermon to write, another chapter in a book to complete.

Don't get me wrong here. I'm not complaining, mind you. I love always having something to do. I love the fact that I am able to choose what I am going to be doing. I cannot imagine what it is like having somebody else telling me what to do. Oh yes, that would be what a husband is all about. Let me just confess my error right here.

Both my wife and I love the work we are doing and often do not even consider it to be work. We just love what we are doing and we love the fact they were able to do it.

But my confession!

It was the last holiday and as usual, I went to my office right after breakfast and began my daily work. For some reason the thought haunted me that this was a holiday and I was probably the only person in the world working.

I shook off that silly thought and got back to work.

I looked at my watch and it was 11 o'clock. One more hour and it would be lunchtime.

One more hour!

Immediately I thought of how much I could accomplish in that one hour and so I set my mind back into the work mode.

I looked at my watch again and it was 11:05 AM. Fifty-five more minutes and it would be lunchtime.

Fifty-five more minutes!

I am not quite sure what happened at the time but I began thinking some rather strange thoughts. Like, who would care if I quit for an early lunch?

It did not take me long to close up shop and head home for an early lunch. When I got there, my wife was rather surprised and told me that lunch was not quite ready yet.

I assured her that I was not in a hurry and went into the living room and sat in my favorite easy chair leaning back and took the snooze-position. For the life of me, I can not understand what happened. It just felt so good just to set there and do nothing.

My wife called me to lunch, we had a very delicious lunch together and my plans were to get back to the office and into work mode.

As I got up to leave I happened to glance in the direction of the living room and saw a lonely easy chair longing for someone to set on her.

"Well," I thought to myself, "just a few minutes of sitting won't do anybody any harm."

So I went and sat down in the chair. It felt so good. An hour went by. Then I convinced myself, "Why not just spend one more hour in this very comfortable chair."

And so my confession. On the last holiday, I absolutely did nothing. I sat in my chair and before I knew it, it was suppertime.

For my confession. I must confess quite sincerely that it really and truly felt good to do nothing for a whole day.

John the beloved understood this when he wrote, "If we confess our sins, he is faithful and just to forgive us *our* sins, and to cleanse us from all unrighteousness" (1 John 1:9).

The experience of God's wonderful forgiveness is based upon my confession.

Chapter 9
Not Smart Enough To Be An Idiot

In my experience, everybody has a slice of "idiot" somewhere hiding inside them. The trick is not to let it show itself at the wrong time.

Since everybody is an idiot to some degree or other, maybe we should not be so hard on people. After all, not everybody is smart enough to be a full blown idiot.

Throughout my life, I have attempted to utilize my "idiot slice" to my own advantage. So far I have had good progress on this aspect of my life, just ask the Gracious Mistress of the Parsonage. With a great deal of affection she will often say, "You are one of the best idiots I have ever known."

Isn't love a wonderful thing?

Although I own up to my "idiot slice" many people for some reason, are not able to do that. After all, if everybody has a slice of idiocy, then what's the problem?

This came to me recently when a small incident happened. I do not quite remember what brought this incident to be, it could be anything these days, but the outcome is what got me.

This guy looked at me with the meanest look, shook his fist at me and said, "Are you an idiot or something?"

Normally I take these things as they come and just move on with my life. But for some reason that "idiot slice" in me kicked into high gear. And I responded, "Which one do you think I am?"

He blinked and said, "Wh-utt?"

So I said, " "Do you think I'm an 'idiot' or a 'something'?"

"After all," I continued, "there is a vast difference between an 'idiot' and a 'something.' What am I?"

That was last week some time and I think he is still trying to figure out what in the world I was talking about. Some people just aren't smart enough to be a plain old idiot.

I believe there is a little bit of intelligence in every idiot. After all, most idiots are smart enough to get a driver's license. And boy, do they drive like idiots.

Just yesterday, I was trying to drive across town and I encountered so many idiots driving that I was tempted to run some of them over. Don't those idiot drivers make you furious?

I know a few people who are simply nuts, but that is a different story altogether. Being an idiot takes a lot of hard work and practice. Not everybody is smart enough to be an idiot.

One driver I encountered, who at first glance I thought was an idiot but he turned out not smart enough to be an idiot. I was driving on my side of the road and going the speed limit. He was behind me and wanted to go faster than the speed limit. That's okay if nobody's in front of you, but I was in front of him and he couldn't get around me.

He honked his horn, hoping, I suppose, that I would get out of his way and let him go. However, I was more of an idiot, so I ignored him. One good thing about being an idiot is that you can ignore people who do not quite come up to the status of being an idiot themselves.

Finally, we got to a place where he could pass me. I just assumed he would pass and that would be the last I would see of him. When he got beside me, he began yelling and screaming and I could not understand anything he was saying.

I did figure out that he must have been a very religious man because he was pointing me to heaven. I guess he was encouraging me to go to heaven. I smiled and shook my head, which only made him a little angrier, for some reason. I did notice though, that the finger he was using to point to heaven was not the finger I would have used. I guess it's a matter of confusion. This guy was not smart enough to be an idiot to know which finger you use to point a person to heaven.

One thing I have discovered about idiots is they are not confined to race, gender or age. You can find idiots anywhere there are people still breathing. An idiot is an equal opportunity engager.

Being an idiot does have its advantages. For example, when my wife sends me to the store to buy some items for the house and I come back with everything but what's on the list I can say, "I just must be an idiot." And, do not let this get back to her, it always works.

If you know who you are and what you are, you can begin using that information to your advantage. If you know you are an idiot then you can bank on that for the rest of your life.

The difference between an idiot and a fool is simply that an idiot is a little short of knowledge. Solomon understood this when he wrote, "The fear of the Lord is the beginning of knowledge: but fools despise wisdom and instruction" (Proverbs 1:7).

And, "The way of a fool is right in his own eyes: but he that hearkeneth unto counsel is wise" (Proverbs 12:15).

I suppose I can't help being an idiot, but I certainly don't have to be a fool as Solomon describes it.

Chapter 10
Apple Fritter: The Fruit Of My Choice

Our country, so it seems, runs on choice. The more choices we have, the better we like it.

Most people in America pride themselves on the ability to make their own choices.

"Freedom of Choice," is the cry you hear all around our country these days. Yet, most people do not have the freedom of choice they think they have. Somebody is influencing the choices they make without them realizing they are being influenced.

That is called marketing.

The Gracious Mistress of the Parsonage and I were watching television the other night, trying to watch a favorite TV program. Finally, from an end of the room that was not my end, came an exasperated sigh. I tried to ignore it, but you know how that works.

The exasperation seemed to accelerate and I knew that if I did not acknowledge it in some way, well, I think you know what would happen.

It was in the middle of some commercials and so I turned to her and said, "What's got you in such pain tonight?" At her age I did not know if there was some medical something or other going on.

"These commercials," she moaned so painfully, "I can't stand all these commercials!"

I must say I was a little bummed out about all the commercials myself. I think every one-hour program is devoted to 30 minutes of commercials. Most of those commercials are for things I have no interest in. Or, they are played at a very inappropriate time. I'm sorry, but I do not love my laxative!

It never fails if we are having our supper while watching television there are 79 commercials for diarrhea. Is this really a major problem in our country today?

Getting back to my wife and the commercials, I responded as cheerfully as I could, "Well, my dear, somebody has to pay for our television viewing privilege."

I felt a cold yet burning stare in my direction.

"Can't they run those lousy commercials when I'm not watching TV?"

Someone once said that silence is Golden and right then I cultivated a golden moment.

Commercials are a way in which manufacturing companies influence our choices. Every product has 100 different companies marketing the same product. I have not done too much research but the little I have done I discovered that the same company makes the same product but sells it under a different name.

There are two categories of products. There is the name brand, which cost a fortune. Then there is the generic brand, which is only a fraction of what the name brand cost. It is the same product, made by the same company, but advertised by difference venues.

This is where choice comes in.

Some people choose the high-priced product because they think it is better.

Some of us choose the low-price product because we know better.

Another night as we were watching television, it seemed most of the commercials had to do with dieting of some kind. There were high calorie diets, low-carb diets and diets that really did not make sense to me.

Watching all of those dieting commercials, I did not see one that I would die for.

Every one of those commercials assumes everybody watching wants to lose 297 pounds. Personally, I have lost the same 5 pounds for over 30 years. I lose 5 pounds and then by golly, three weeks later I find those 5 pounds, at least they recognize me.

Anybody can lose weight; it is all a matter of choice. Personally, I do not plan to lose any sleep because I cannot lose weight. I think it is going to be rather funny if when we go to heaven everybody is fat. Wouldn't that be something? We plummet ourselves almost to death trying to lose weight and get to heaven and everybody is fat.

It all boils down to choice and the fact that most people think they are making their own choices.

Those of us who are on the husband side of the marital equation know we do not make our own choices. Our choices are made for us by our "better half." Why do you think we get married?

My wife is a great one for fruit and vegetables. Every day of our life is fruit and vegetables. To mix things up a little bit one day it will be vegetables and fruit.

She prepares the fruit and then invites me to make a choice. I am sure she did not see all of this in any television commercial; at least I hope she hasn't. She is proud of the display of fruit choices she has for me.

She is also concerned about my diet. Much more than I am. I do not think my diet is so important that both of us should be concerned about it. If she chooses to be concerned about my diet, that is her choice.

I choose to be a little more cavalier when it comes to dieting.

Actually, and do not tell her I said this, but my fruit of choice is the humble Apple fritter. It has everything my heart desires and a few things my body desires, too.

I like with David said, "Delight thyself also in the LORD; and he shall give thee the desires of thine heart" (Psalms 37:4 KJV).

It is all a matter of choice, that is, making the right choice.

Chapter 11
The Squirrel And Birds Controversy

I have learned controversy is what life is really all about. Controversy means there is two sides, one side has no idea what the other side is thinking. Of course, there are those controversies when neither side is actually doing any thinking. That is what is called politics.

I had an illustration of this recently. The Gracious Mistress of the Parsonage and I spent a wonderful week's vacation in Ohio visiting our son and his family. It is always great to spend time with family.

Early in the morning, I would go to the front porch, sit down with a book and casually enjoy the quietness. One particular morning as I was marinating in the silence, I heard what sounded like an explosion in the tree.

I looked and saw a squirrel racing down the tree followed by two screaming birds. I watched as the squirrel disappeared into some bushes in front of the fence that bordered the property. I could see him standing and staring at the birds who were screaming at him.

He stood like a frozen monument, they finally gave up and flew back up the tree and I saw them go to their nest.

I looked over and saw the squirrel standing there staring up at the tree in the area where the nest was.

I almost went back to my book when I saw out of the corner my eye the squirrel leaping off the fence and racing back up the tree towards the nest.

Almost immediately, the birds that were guarding the nest exploded in anger and chased the squirrel back down the tree and he jumped into the bushes and hid from them. They squawked and screamed for a few moments, threatening some very bad business to the squirrel.

Again, he stood there just staring.

This went on about six times before I finally realized what was going on.

The birds were up there protecting their eggs, which would soon hatch into little birdies. They were protecting their family and their future.

The squirrel, on the other hand, saw in that nest up the tree a fresh scrambled egg delicacy. The controversy was between a now pleasure and a future family. If only the squirrel and the birds could come together and talk out their controversy, maybe they could have come to some reasonable resolution.

Of course, it would be rather difficult to talk the squirrel out of enjoying a scrumptious little meal.

That reminded me of some controversies we have had in the parsonage through the years. It all boils down to the squirrel and the birds' controversy. I want something now, just like a squirrel, and my wife, like those two birds, is one of those people that know how to plan for the future. For me, I am not sure how long I am going to live, so I want something right now!

I am a little squirrelly along this line.

I do remember a time when my wife was preparing cookies for Christmas. My wife cannot do anything at the last minute. It takes her time to prepare and plan all of her cooking. So, when it comes to Christmas cookies she is beginning the preparation long before Thanksgiving.

It was the beginning of December, if I remember correctly, and my wife was baking a bunch of cookies that she was going to use to give to certain people for Christmas. Unfortunately, I do not pay attention much to things like that. I came into the kitchen and discovered to my delight, that there were cookies on the counter but no wife in the kitchen.

I was only going to take one with the belief that she would not miss just one cookie. That was my original plan. My plans never have a long-range effect like hers do. My plans are always in the "NOW."

That cookie was so delicious, so scrumptious, that I thought it deserved one more cookie for my consumption. After all, she would not miss two cookies. As I said, I live in the "NOW" and I am not quite sure how many cookies I consumed before my wife came into the kitchen.

All I know is, there was squawking and pretty soon she was chasing me not only out of the kitchen but out of the house shouting, "How dare you eat all of those cookies. They're not for you!"

Getting back to the porch, the squirrel and the birds, I began to feel a little bit of empathy for the squirrel. I knew exactly what he was going through.

Controversies are like that. One side believes one way and the other side believes another way and the twain shall never meet. There is the bird's nest view and there is the fence view. Not to mention, the cookies in the kitchen view.

My wife saw that one way, while I saw them completely differently. It is really not my fault. If my wife did not make the cookies so delicious, I would not be tempted to eat them. In fact, they are so delicious that you cannot just eat one. Or, at least I can't.

Thinking about that I was reminded what the prophet said, "Can two walk together, except they be agreed?" (Amos 3:3).

I know some controversies cannot be settled, but I think a good relationship deserves coming to some point of agreement.

Chapter 12
How Many Mondays Are There In One Week?

I must admit I am not up to date with all of the technology and gadgets today. Just when I think I have something mastered, they upgrade it or replace it with something that I cannot figure out. I guess that is why God gave grandfathers grandchildren.

It started on a Monday morning and I thought I would use the latest technology and order something online from Staples and then go over and pick it up. I would save a lot of time and it would look like I knew what I was doing. I love it when a plan comes together.

I must say it was very easy to give them my money online, just a little too easy for my comfort.

Then I went to Staples to pick up my order. When I got there, unfortunately, I had ordered the wrong product. I wanted black ink and I ordered, by mistake, colored ink. I had plenty of colored ink but I was completely out of black ink.

When I found out that I had made this error, I was beside myself. Believe me, standing beside me is no picnic.

I went to the customer window and explained to them my problem, which they were most gracious to help me with and cancel the order and refund my money. Being elated I then went and picked up the black ink that I wanted for my printer.

I do love it when a plan comes together.

I remember my grandmother saying, "As your Monday starts, so shall your week end." Driving back to my office, I chuckled to myself thinking that maybe good old grandmother was wrong on this one.

Getting to my office, I began to put the ink cartridge in my printer only to find out that, although I had black ink, I had the wrong ink cartridge! When will Monday end!

I started out the day trying to save time and trips, now I had to go back to the store and exchange the wrong cartridge for the right one. I am not sure, but I think I heard some snickering behind the customer window, but I refused to look in their direction. They can keep their snickers to themselves.

Driving back from the store I thought again of my dear old grandmother. Perhaps, looking at my experience today, she was absolutely right.

When I got back to the office, I remembered I had an appointment to take my truck in for a check up and new tires. So, back into town I went thinking about dear old grandmother.

The end result of the truck inspection was to cost me an arm and a leg. How do they expect me to drive my truck without an arm or a leg?

I was so happy when Monday was over thinking that the worst of my week concluded.

The next day I had a doctor's visit. It was one of those annual visits that you have to take so that the doctor can feel good about his doctoring. As much as he examines me, he can never find anything wrong with me. I am sure glad he is not a psychiatrist.

As he was looking at his chart, he looked up at me and said, "You haven't had a blood test in over a year." With one of those Dr. smiles he said, "I'll have my nurse set up an appointment for you."

Of course, it would have to be the next day because of what they call their "fasting rules." I asked the nurse if that included coffee. Of course, it did and then I said, "Are you sure you want to see me before I have my morning coffee?"

I came in the next morning feeling a little nervous because, one, I didn't have my morning coffee, and two, Ms. Dracula was going to poke me with a needle the size of the Empire State building and suck all the blood out of my body. Talk about being a nervous wreck!

Stumbling out of the doctor's office, I headed for my truck and drove directly to McDonald's to get my morning coffee.

I settled down in my office and began to think that this week is over as far as the problems are concerned. As I drove home for lunch, I noticed the new wheels on the truck shivered and so I had to take it back and have them check it.

Every once in a while, I have a week where every day is Monday and this week seems to be one of those weeks. My grandmother certainly was right. As your week begins, so shall it end. My prayer was that it would end very quickly.

I would like to see a week that has no Monday in it at all, but that is not going to happen.

My grandmother was trying to explain to me that there are no perfect days. Some days may be better than other days, but there are really no perfect days for us. Just when you think you got everything organized, something happens that puts everything in a disheveled mess.

Solomon spoke of a perfect day. "But the path of the just *is* as the shining light, that shineth more and more unto the perfect day" (Proverbs 4:18).

Everybody has their definition of a perfect day, but I choose to rest in God's definition of a perfect day.

Chapter 13
Pinching Pennies In A Nickel Economy

An incident happened this past week that created for me a certain pause to think about things.

I don't often think about too many things. After all, with only one little gray cell, it is hard to think about things in the plural. "One-thought-at-a-time," is my life motto. Experience has taught me that too many thoughts at any given time, usually leads to trouble with the Gracious Mistress of the Parsonage.

I was going to pick up a few items at Publix when it happened. I parked in the parking lot as normal, got out of the car and started towards the store. Halfway to the store is when it happened.

Even now as I think about it, I'm a little excited. Believe me; it takes quite a bit to get me excited these days.

Walking towards the entrance to the store, I saw on the ground a penny, which caused me to stop in my tracks.

I do not bend over for anything unless it is important these days. My problem is that if I bend over I will have difficulty in unbending. It has to be something rather important for me to bend down, let alone pick it up.

However, there it was in all of its glory.

I do remember one of my favorite quotes from Benjamin Franklin, "A penny saved is a penny earned." He was a wise old man and should know about these things.

I would like to amend that quote by saying, "A penny found is a penny earned." After all, you cannot leave a penny there on the ground all by itself.

Some people would complain that a penny is not worth that much. But a penny is worth one cent. And one cent has value, at least in my pocket.

The formula goes something like this: 100 pennies equals one dollar. 100 dollars equals a whole heap of money.

As I bent down to pick up this orphaned penny, I thought of all the other orphaned pennies that I have collected throughout my life. I make it a practice to adopt all of these orphaned pennies and keep them safely on my dresser.

The penny that I picked up was a little corroded and dirty, but it had the same value as a bright shiny clean penny. Outside appearances do not fool me. In fact, I will take all the dirty pennies you have.

I don't know if it was my upbringing that caused me to be rather cautious with money. Or, if not having a lot of money throughout life has done the same thing. What I do know is, I am very careful when it comes to money.

Don't get me wrong. Money is not my god. Some people make a god out of money, which I think is rather silly. Money cannot create a God, but it is interesting that God can create money?

As a young boy, my father taught me this one thing, "Son, if you can't afford something you don't need it." I think he was right about 95% of the time. Then there are those times when I really needed something and could not afford it.

I have tried to save money. I own a small piggy bank that I put extra cash into it as I find it. I try to hide it from my wife, which is never a good thing. If you have been married as long as I have, you will conclude that there is actually no way to hide anything from your wife.

I was trying to save up a little cash for special things that I will leave unsaid at this point. Whenever I got a new coin, I would put it in this little piggy bank I had hidden in my closet.

I almost reached my goal when something happened. I went to get some money out of the little piggy bank only to find it empty. Now what do I do? Do I let somebody in the house know that I've had a secret stash in my closet? Do I now come out of the closet?

I figured the best protocol would be to say nothing and therefore not get into any trouble. Well, you know how that goes.

That evening as we were watching a little TV my wife happened to say, "I hope you don't mind, but I took some of the money out of your piggy bank in the closet to buy some items."

Don't mind? Even if I did mind, I really can't say anything. All I could say was, "That's okay, I was just saving it for a rainy day."

"That's what I thought," my wife said most thoughtfully, "yesterday was a rainy day."

At least my money was used for somebody's good purpose. The thought that danced around in my head was, how long did she know I had that piggy bank in the closet?

So, the penny that I found in the parking lot this week has found a nice residence in my piggy bank, that is, until it rains.

The apostle Paul said it best, "For the love of money is the root of all evil: which while some coveted after, they have erred from the faith, and pierced themselves through with many sorrows" (1 Timothy 6:10).

Money certainly has its place, but not in the first place where God belongs.

Chapter 14
Thoughts, Plots And Other Dangerous Activities

One day this past week, I got up a little earlier than usual and to keep from waking up the Gracious Mistress of the Parsonage I got my coffee and went to the back porch to enjoy a quiet early morning.

As I sat on the back porch drinking my coffee and taking in the early morning atmosphere, I noticed a bunch of birds sitting on the fence in the backyard. They were squawking at me as though I was the worst person in their world. I believe what they were screaming about was that I had not filled the bird feeder yet.

I screeched back at them and they only looked at me quizzically and kept on squawking. Obviously, they could not understand my accent.

Watching them for a few moments, I began to think. That is a very dangerous thing to do, especially so early in the morning and especially with a hot cup of coffee in your hand.

I began thinking about the fact that whenever I put the feed in the bird feeder none of the birds ever come and thank me for it. However, when I do not put feed in the birdfeeder they squawk and yell at me as though I had committed the unpardonable sin.

That's gratitude for you.

I tried explaining that I would put feed in the bird feeder when I got around to it. But right now, I explained, I'm just enjoying a quiet moment with my cup of coffee. Now, could you just leave me alone for a moment? And, quit all this fowl language.

I took another long sip of coffee and began reflecting more about this and how this was very typical of people. They complain when they don't get what they want, but when they get what they want rarely do they thank anybody. Their assumption is that they deserve what they want.

It reminded me of an incident in the life of Jesus when he healed 10 lepers. Only one of those lepers ever came back to thank Jesus for what he did. That seems to be very typical.

How much of what I expect do I really deserve?

Thinking about this brought me to the place of trying to figure out some little plot against these birds in my backyard. If they are not thankful for what I give them and if they are screeching at me when they do not get what they want, what could I do to get even with these little feathered rascals?

As I continued sipping my coffee, my brain was running at high speed trying to figure out how I could trick these birds into being a little more appreciative of what I do for them. After all, if I did not feed them they would not get fed.

One thought I had was I could put feed in the bird feeder and then tape shut all of the openings so that they could see the feed but they couldn't get to it. I liked that idea. Oh, how it would make them so aggravated to see all that food there and not able to get to it.

The more I thought about this idea the more devious my thinking became.

What if I would build something, like a trap, and put feed in the inside so that when they tried to get to it they would be trapped and could not get out. I could watch them and laugh and laugh and laugh.

They could not get to the feed and they could not get out of the feeder. Oh, how I liked that idea.

Soon my mind was putting out plot after plot getting even with these rascally, feathered minions teaching them a lesson or two. I was so impressed with all of these plots that I had to get a paper and pencil and start jotting them down. This was serious with me.

Suddenly, I heard a quiet voice from inside the door saying, "What are you doing so early?"

Looking around, there my wife stood at the door looking at me with the strangest of looks. I have seen strange looks from her, but this was the strangest.

It shocked me back into reality and for a brief moment, I almost told her what I was doing. I knew if I did that, I would be in deep trouble.

Coming up with a fresh plot I simply said, "I'm just enjoying the quietness of the morning."

"I think," she said, "I'll come out and join you and together we can enjoy the quietness of the morning."

All my thoughts and plots came to an abrupt end.

Then she said, "I wonder why those birds over there on that fence are looking this way and squawking?"

For a moment I thought I would explain it to her, but then I figured out she probably would not get the whole story. Or at least, she would wonder why in the world I was talking to birds. Then she would suggest that it was because I had a "birdbrain." That suggestion has come up quite a few times.

The apostle Paul stated it this way, "Casting down imaginations, and every high thing that exalteth itself against the knowledge of God, and bringing into captivity every thought to the obedience of Christ" (2 Corinthians 10:5).

When my thoughts focus on Christ, it lifts me above my circumstances.

Chapter 15
Bad Breath Ain't Always That Bad

I am always super sensitive about my breath. I try to take care of it, but at times, I'm a little bit off schedule. I really do not know when my breath is really bad.

For me, I only know my breath is bad when the person standing in front of me passes out.

It is rather embarrassing to have bad breath, particularly when you are in the company of very sophisticated people. I have bad breath all the time because of my great delight in eating cheese. The Gracious Mistress of the Parsonage warns me all the time that eating cheese will create bad breath. I know she is right, but cheese is very delicious.

I was boarding an airplane to travel north when the thought struck me that I had eaten a block of cheese before I got to the airport. I was wondering if my breath smelled bad or not. I tried to test it on myself but it never registered with my nose.

I know I have a nose, but my nose does not know when to smell anything. The only thing my nose does for me is sneeze, particularly when I am not prepared. So, I can't smell things the way my wife does. She can smell an odor seven days before it is produced!

How she does that I will never know and at my stage in life I am never going to ask her.

According to her, bad breath is always bad, which is why they call it "bad breath." My contention is, bad is a relative thing. One person smells one way, another person smells the other way and the twain shall never collide. What is bad for one person may not be bad for another person.

I have a habit of nibbling on cheese. At times, my wife thinks that I am just a mouse. Actually, she uses the word "rat," but that is a different story. I just love cheese. When I come home the first thing I do is go to the refrigerator, get out a block of cheese, slice it, go sit down and enjoy nibbling on that cheese never concerned about the bad breath it might create.

My wife is very conscious of this and always carries with her a packet of breath mints. Whenever she offers me a breath mint, I know that she smells my bad breath. I take a breath mint just to console her, but it really does not make any difference to me.

My contention is, bad breath isn't always that bad.

Getting back to my plane ride. As I was boarding the plane, I remembered I indulged in my slice of cheese. At first, I was a little worried because on the plane you almost sit on top of one another.

Fortunately, when I got to my row of seats I was the first one and so I was able to sit near the window. One of the things I enjoy in flying is leaning back and resting in the quietness of the atmosphere. However, most of the time I have somebody seated next to me that does not know the meaning of silence.

As I was getting situated in my seat, somebody came and took the seat next to me. Before they could even sit down and buckle their seatbelt, their mouth started jabbering. If there is anything I do not like it is a mouth that jabbers and jabbers without quitting.

I am quite familiar with the English language, but I am always perplexed at how somebody can talk without stopping or even pausing for a "period."

Seated next to me was such a person. From the moment he got in, he began talking and for the life of me I could never figure out what he was talking about. He went from one subject to the next subject without even a bridge between the two.

The flight was a 2½-hour flight and I was not sure how in the world I was going to endure such endless chatter all the way. It's not so much that I mind someone else chattering, it's the fact that while there chattering they never give me an opportunity to chatter back.

While I was sitting there, an idea came to mind. I don't always have good ideas, but I think this one was pristine in every sense of the word. I began to think of that slice of cheese I had nibbled before boarding the airplane. If my wife is correct, and she usually is, my breath at this time would be dangerously stinky, to use her phrase.

With a smile on my face, I turned to the chatterbox and just let out very slowly my bad breath in his direction. It must've been bad because all of a sudden, he stopped and he could not breathe. Just to make sure it was working, I sent another hot breath in his direction. His eyes crossed and he set back and looked in the other direction. He had nothing more to say.

I do not think Job had this in mind when he wrote, "The spirit of God hath made me, and the breath of the Almighty hath given me life" (Job 33:4).

God's breath is not bad, but it is good to the point of giving me his life to live.

Chapter 16
Where Have All The Clowns Gone?

The Gracious Mistress of the Parsonage and I were getting ourselves situated in the living room with some after supper coffee while watching a little bit of TV. These days, a little bit of TV is about all a person can handle.

Nothing quite measures up to a nice hot cup of coffee after a scrumptious supper and if anybody can scrumpturize a supper, it is the Gracious Mistress of the Parsonage. Every once in a while she will point out the fact that I am not as skinny as I once was. My response to her is simply this, "It's your fault for being such a wonderful cook."

That stops the conversation; she smiles, sits back and thinks about what I just said. I sit back and smile thinking that I have gotten out of another bit of a pickle.

It is very hard to keep up with the news today because we have such technology that whatever happens anywhere in the universe we have an immediate story about it.

I do not know about anybody else, but I am just a little bit tired of the news these days. My wife and I were shocked this week to see a news report about, of all things, clowns. These clowns, so the reporter went on, were scaring people and committing crimes like robbery.

Really?

Then they had some footage of somebody dressed up as a clown, frightening people and threatening to do bodily harm. Now, some places are forbidding clowns to show up. Even during the Halloween season, some stores are not selling clown costumes.

How far have we gone in our culture when clowns are a threat to our culture?

It was not always that way. In high school, for example, I was often referred to as the class clown. That was a title of deep reverence and pride. To be the class clown meant you were doing things that made other people laugh. You were joking and clowning around and creating a great deal of merriment. With the tension many of our high school teachers created in class, the class clown had an important job of bringing down the tension.

If there were awards for being the class clown, I certainly would have gotten one in high school. They only have awards for scholarship and athletics. I say nothing is more important in a class than the class clown. There should be some kind of recognition in this area.

Then when I was growing up, my mother kept telling me to, "Stop clowning around!"

At the time, I really did not understand what she was trying to say. In high school, it was a measure of acceptance, but in the home, it was something inappropriate.

Although I do respect my mother, I have yet to "stop clowning around."

Now, I have my wife telling me to, "Stop clowning around." I have often wondered if this is not some kind of gene passed on to every woman.

There was not just one news story about these fallacious clowns doing all sorts of criminal activity, but it seemed to be as if a trend was developing.

I have a friend of mine who is a professional clown and does all kinds of work with children's and charity activities. You would not find a nicer person in all the world than my good clown friend. I have not talked to him about this new development in clownville, but I am sure he has a good take on it.

The purpose of the clown is to make people laugh. That's all.

Now even a certain fast food chain has given their clown a vacation until some of this nonsense passes over. I think this is stupid.

I believe that if somebody is misusing the clown motif for "naughty activities," the people who are affected the most should justly punish him. And by that, I mean children and people who still are acting like children.

If any of these people dressed in a clown outfit should be caught doing something that is unclownish there should be some very dire circumstances administered in an appropriate way. Like a pie in the face.

At one time, no circus was complete without a whole bunch a clowns keeping the merriment going strong. All of these false clowns should be gathered together and dealt with rather brutishly. After all, if you are going to defame such a sacred character in the American culture, you need to be dealt with very severely. How dare somebody do this sort of thing to an iconic figure of American society?

Why is it we have some people who will take something that is very precious to certain people, turn it around and make it a very negative and nasty thing? There should be a law against that sort of thing. Where is the politician that is going to put his or her foot down against this kind of travesty in our society?

Is nothing sacred anymore in our country? I think the apostle Paul had something like this in mind when he wrote, "Unto the pure all things *are* pure: but unto them that are defiled and unbelieving *is* nothing pure; but even their mind and conscience is defiled" (Titus 1:15).

Why will some people take something that other people get pleasure from and turn it into something negative? Only a corrupt mind would do this.

Chapter 17
How Did The Devil Get My Cell Phone Number?

I am not one easily rattled. When I am rattled, look out for anything can happen.

For the most part, I try to stay calm, cool and collected. Then there are times when I have had enough and I am not going to take it anymore.

When I am rattled about something, it is not small or insignificant. I can swat pesky little bugs all of my life and never get rattled by a bug.

Lately, some things have been developing "in my world," that has me more than a little concerned. In fact, it is bordering on the territory of being rattled. Something needs to be done because if I am rattled in this area, look out!

I am not sure if I am just now noticing it or if it has been here for a while. When I got my cell phone I was under the impression the only people who would have my cell phone number would be those I gave it to. I am not one to give out my cell phone number to just anybody. If you have my cell phone number, you are in a high-level category of BFFs.

I believe sincerely that the devil has hacked into my cell phone, collected my cell phone number and is selling my number to the most despicable people he owns.

Lately, I have been getting political calls. People trying to interview me concerning the up coming election. They want me to contribute to political polls being evaluated. They want my opinion and they have a whole slew of questions they are going to be asking me.

I know they do not want my opinion because all of these calls are what is called Robo calls. In other words, it is not an actual person asking these questions, but rather a machine. If you think for one moment that I am going to carry on a conversation with some machine, you do not have all your wires connected.

How they get my cell phone number, is beyond me. It probably is their close connection with the devil himself.

I have also been getting calls from some company that feels I am in some sort of pain. They call and say I requested on their website this pain solution. Now, what they want to know is it my back pain, or elbow pain, or a knee pain?

I have been so fed up with these calls that I finally said, "I do have a pain in the neck." To which, I got an excited reply as to how they could help my pain in the neck.

You know what's coming. I told them that the pain in my neck was them calling me and if they want to help this pain in the neck go away to stop calling me, for Pete's sake.

I just about had it with this. The question I wrestle with is, should I lie to these people calling me?

For instance. Somebody called me last week telling me they noticed a certain virus on my computer and if I would allow them access to my computer they could fix my computer. Talk about a pain in the neck!

This was about the 15th time this company called me offering to fix my computer. So, I thought if they are going to waste my time by calling me, maybe I should waste their time by trying to get them to fix my computer.

"Oh yes," I said as excited as I could sound, "please fix my computer for me."

Now they wanted me to turn my computer on and so forth and so on. I must confess that at the time I wasn't near my computer, I was on my cell phone.

They gave me instructions and I obeyed them, or at least I told him I was obeying them.

"All right," I said, "My computer is on, what do I do next?" I will confess to you if you promise not to tell anybody, but I did not have my computer on.

Then they gave me instructions that I was to go to a certain website.

"Okay," I said, "I'm there, what do I do now?"

They gave me a password I was supposed to use to get access to them so they could get access to my computer.

"Have you done it yet?"

"Yes, I punched it in and what I do next?"

"Something's wrong," the person at the other end of the phone said. "You must not have put in the right password. Let me give it to you again."

He gave it to me again, which in turn I gave it back to him, again.

This went on for about 20 minutes and the person on the other end of my cell phone was getting very frustrated and borderline angry. I, on the other end of the cell phone, could hardly control my laughter.

By the time he hung up, he was very frustrated and could not understand why it was not working.

After this person hung up on me and I quit laughing, I thought of what David said. "Give them according to their deeds, and according to the wickedness of their endeavours: give them after the work of their hands; render to them their desert" (Psalms 28:4).

Sometimes giving back what you get can bring you to a certain level of joy you did not have before.

Chapter 18
Apart From That, I'm Doing Fine!

I know I am not correct on many things, just ask the Gracious Mistress of the Parsonage. If I could be right as many times as I am wrong, I would be a genius. The problem is, I am more wrong than I am right, which puts me a little bit out of balance.

People always say things they really do not mean. I guess they are just trying to be nice and courteous.

For instance. My wife will say as I leave the door to go somewhere, "Drive safely."

I do not know what that means. Does she think I am going to drive like an idiot? Well, maybe that is not a good illustration.

Another one is, if you are going to a party someone will say, "Have fun."

Does that mean they are under the impression that you are not going to have fun unless you are enticed? Why do people always say things like that?

We always say things that we do not mean.

Of course, I am always a little guarded about certain things my wife may say to me. The most infamous one would be, "Does this dress make me look fat?" I am not sure who came up with that one, but their head was not spinning in the right direction.

After thinking about that for a little bit I am under the impression that if anyone asks me that question, particularly if it is my wife, they are not looking for the right answer. They are looking for a compliment.

Is it more important to tell the truth or to encourage someone? That has always been my dilemma.

One question has bugged me for a long time. I must confess that I have done it myself, but it still bugs me. It is when we meet somebody and say, "Hello, how are you doing?"

Why do we say something like that? Whenever I ask somebody how they are doing, I really do not want them to tell me how they are doing. I am trying to be courteous and friendly. I do not want to know the details of their life.

As I said, I find myself saying the very same thing. I am trying to get over this phrase-addiction and probably need several months in some rehabilitation center. It would be worth it to get this out of my conversation.

I do not know if I was just having a bad day or if I was just fed up with this question. Not long ago I was coming out of the grocery store and somebody greeted me and said, "Hello, how are you doing today?"

Something came over me. To this day I cannot explain what in the world made me do what I did. But I did it and there it is.

I could tell the person who asked the question was in a hurry to get into the grocery store but I did it anyway. He asked me how I was and so I stopped him and told him how I was.

"I'm glad you asked," I started, "because I'm not feeling very well today." I noticed he was trying to get beyond me, but I was going to have my say no matter what.

"I hurt my big toe this morning, I think I broke a toenail. I've been limping all day long and I'm getting rather tired of it."

He looked at me and then glanced at the grocery store, but I pretended as if I did not see.

"I got up this morning," I continued as though I had nothing else in the world to do, "with my back hurting so much I could hardly get out of bed. I'm not so sure what happened, but boy does it really hurt."

He looked at his watch and then looked at the grocery store entrance again, but I continued to pretend I did not see it.

"My day hasn't gone very well," I complained to him, "I just seem to be late for everything. I missed my appointment at the doctor this morning and I'm not sure when I'm going to get back to see that doctor."

I could see he was getting very nervous and borderline agitated. He tried to interrupt me, but I pretended I did not notice.

"I don't know what I'm gonna do with my car. There's a big noise rattling in the engine and I'm not sure if I should take it in or what I should do with it."

"Well," he said rather anxiously, "I gotta get into the store." With that, he briskly walked away muttering.

I am sure he talked about that all they long to his friends. He probably thought I was crazy. Sometimes it is good to be crazy. After all, he is the one that asked me how I was. If he did not want to know how I was, why did he ask me how I was?

I chuckled to myself and then I got thinking about my prayer life. I wonder how many times I do that in my prayer life. I pray about something, but I really am not that interested in it.

I wonder if Jesus had this in mind when he said, "And all things, whatsoever ye shall ask in prayer, believing, ye shall receive" (Matthew 21:22).

Prayer is not meaningless gibberish, but faith-focused asking.

Chapter 19
The Sound Of Crickets Chirping In The Backyard

Noise has become a daily experience for many people today. From morning until night, we are surrounded by noise of all kinds. People have gotten accustomed to an atmosphere of noise. For my part, I am just a little bit tired of all the noise. What would life be like if there was silence?

The Gracious Mistress of the Parsonage and I were relaxing on the back porch after supper, drinking our coffee and enjoying the evening. Nothing quite compares to drinking coffee on the back porch after a hard day. Then my wife said something that startled me.

"Do you hear that?"

I listened and strained my ears but I could not hear anything. If my wife says there is something to hear, then there is something to hear. I strained my ears as much as possible, but to no effect.

"Don't you hear that?" She said once more.

For the life of me, I did not hear anything and was beginning to think she was trying to pull one over on me. She does that occasionally and catches me. She thinks it's rather funny, although I laugh along with her, I am not laughing on the inside.

Finally, I said, "What are you talking about? I don't hear anything."

She was staring across the backyard as though she was looking at something.

"Don't you hear that silence?"

Personally, I did not know you could hear silence, but I was not going to argue with her at the time. I stared in the direction she was staring and still could not figure out what she was talking about.

Then it came to me.

Across our backyard several crickets were chirping. Normally I do not hear those crickets, but I could hear them loud and clear from where I was setting. What they were singing I am not quite sure, but I enjoyed listening to them at the time. It sounded so serene and peaceful.

Sometimes our life is so crowded with other things that we do not hear some of the more quiet things. The noise around us crowds out some of the quietness in our life.

"Okay," I said with a grin, "I hear the silence now."

I suppose crickets chirp all the time, particularly the ones in our backyard, but I do not always hear it. For the next hour, my wife and I quietly listened to those crickets chirping and we enjoyed every moment of it.

"Isn't that silence," my wife whispered, "truly refreshing?"

I do not always agree with my wife, but this time I was in complete harmony with her thoughts. It is refreshing to listen to silence that has absolutely no agenda but to quiet the mind.

Out in our society, we have noise and activity and miss the good things in life. I just wonder how many people miss the things in life that are truly refreshing because of all of the noise and activity around.

It takes some time to get used to the silence, but my wife and I, as we sipped our evening coffee and staring across the backyard, enjoyed the sounds of silence.

To appreciate the silence is one of the great privileges of life. I must confess I do not often get the chance to enjoy silence, especially hearing the chirping of the crickets in the backyard.

As we were sitting there just enjoying the silence, I could not help but think of one startling little question. Why in the world did God create crickets? Of what purpose do they have in this busy world of ours?

Very few people get the chance to hear crickets chirping, so why in the world would God take the time and effort to create them?

If you would ask somebody when was the last time they heard crickets chirping, I am sure you would get the silent treatment from them. Nobody really takes the time to think about crickets let alone listen to them. We have too much to do and too many other things to listen to, to spend our time listening to silence.

"Don't you," my wife sighed deeply, "just love those crickets?"

I was not going to argue with my wife. I have never given crickets much thought in the past, but as we sat there, I began to appreciate the sounds of crickets in the evening.

After a few moments of silence, I replied, "We ought to spend more time listening to those crickets."

I should not say this, but we named those crickets. One was Albert and the other we called Beatrice. Why? Does it really matter?

From then on whenever we wanted to enjoy a little bit of quietness one of us would say, "How about an A and B concert?" We always knew what that meant; time to spend on the back porch enjoying the cricket concert.

It takes a lot of discipline to get to the place to enjoy silence. For my part, I want to hear everything and know everything that is going on around me. It is as though I need to approve everything that has happened.

Thinking about this I thought about David. Maybe this is what he meant when he wrote, "Be still, and know that I *am* God: I will be exalted among the heathen, I will be exalted in the earth" (Psalms 46:10).

I am ready for another A and B concert this evening.

Chapter 20
The Only Contest I Really Win Each Year

Between now and the end of the year our house is going to be a mad dash for the stores in preparation for Christmas.

This time of the year, I lay low and try to be as invisible as possible. If I hide in the shadows of the parsonage and do not speak, I am in pretty good shape. I have been practicing this for over 40 years, so I have reached a certain level of proficiency.

Having a wife and two daughters has been a challenge, especially at this time of the year. My son and I have survived and so I am sure I will make it through another year. However, I am not taking anything for granted.

I am somewhat of a competitive person in some degree. I like a good challenge and I certainly like to win. Going up against the Gracious Mistress of the Parsonage has not been a successful competition. Even when she loses, so to speak, she wins. When she wins, I also win, so why should I complain?

The contest at this time of the year is to see how much money these ladies of the parsonage can save. I have not kept track over the years for obvious reasons, so I do not know who is ahead and who is behind.

I would not say that they were Shopaholics, but I am pretty sure they are. From my point of view, I am in no position to challenge them on this serious addiction. To challenge them thusly, would require several weeks in a rehabilitation center for myself. Who wants to go there during the holidays?

I try not to keep track, but I believe it all begins with what is called "Black Friday." I am not sure why it is called "Black Friday" because after it is all over my checkbook is in deep red.

On this audacious holiday, if it can be called a holiday, I keep out of their way.

They will start early in the morning and throughout the day they will come home to unload and boast to me about how much money they saved. Then, off they go back on the shopping trail. For my part, I would never want to stand between them and their shopping destination because, I just have grown accustomed to living.

Although I am not much into shopping, I know when to shop and when not to shop. The purpose of my shopping is not to see how much I can save. If I want to save money, I will stay home and drink a nice hot cup of coffee.

Halfway through the shopping season, my wife and I were sitting in the living room drinking our evening coffee and she was explaining to me her shopping plan. The more she talked the less I understood. I did not know you needed a plan to go shopping. My plan is very simple, do not go shopping!

I happen to notice that one of our spare bedrooms was getting rather full of her shopping items. I just walked by the bedroom, glanced in and quickly walked down the hall as far away as possible. If there is one thing I do not want to do around this time of year, it is wrapping Christmas presents.

One year I was enticed into wrapping Christmas presents, I did such a bad job, I was never invited to do it again. I will not say in public that I did that on purpose. I just will say, I love it when a plan comes together.

As we were relaxing in the living room, my wife began explaining how much money she saved this year in shopping. I listened for as long as I could. I do not know how much she saved, just what she told me. It is almost like a contest with her to see how much money she can save each year.

The biggest challenge is to try to out save her and the two daughters. They have been taught by the best and yet I am not sure they have ever beaten her in this one contest.

When there was a little lull in the conversation, I sneaked a the little question of my own.

"How much," I queried as seriously as possible, "have you saved so far in your shopping?"

I thought it was rather an innocent question to present at the time.

"How much," she said with a very serious look, "I saved over $300 so far." With that, she set back in her chair and smiled. $300 is a lot of money you have to admit.

Then I pop this one, "How much have you spent so far?"

After some thought and a quick look into her checkbook, she came up with the figure, $700.

She informed me that her savings were almost half of what she spent.

There was a moment when I was tempted to challenge this contest by saying, "Well, I saved $700 by not shopping."

On second thought, would it be worth it? Sometimes it is better to concede and have everybody happy, than to win and be the only one that is happy.

Solomon understood this when he wrote, "A fool uttereth all his mind: but a wise *man* keepeth it in till afterwards" (Proverbs 29:11).

My goal in life, particularly as a husband, is to be a wise man.

Chapter 21
Four Things God Wants You to Know

1. <u>**You Need To Be Saved**</u>
   - "Except a man be born again, he cannot see the kingdom of God." (John 3:3)
   - "For all have sinned and come short of the glory of God." (Romans 3:23)
   - "There is not a just man upon earth, that doeth good, and sinneth not." (Ecclesiastes 7:20)
   - "We are all as an unclean thing, and all our righteousnesses are as filthy rags." (Isaiah 64:6)

2. <u>**You Cannot Save Yourself**</u>
   - "Not by works of righteousness which we have done, but according to his mercy he saved us." (Titus 3:5)
   - "By the works of the law shall no flesh be justified." (Galatians 2:16)
   - "For whosoever shall keep the whole law, and yet offend in one point, he is guilty of all." (James 2:10)

- "There is a way which seemeth right unto a man, but the end thereof are the ways of death." (Proverbs 14:12)

3. Jesus Has Already Provided For Your Salvation

- "Who [Jesus] his own self bare our sins in his own body on the tree, that we, being dead to sins, should live unto righteousness." (1 Peter 2:24)
- "For Christ also hath once suffered for sins, the just for the unjust, that he might bring us to God." (1 Peter 3:18)
- "For God so loved the world, that he gave his only begotten Son, that whosoever believeth in him should not perish, but have everlasting life." (John 3:16)

4. Jesus Will Enable You to Overcome Temptation

- "The Lord knoweth how to deliver the godly out of temptations, and to reserve the unjust unto the day of judgment to be punished." (2 Peter 2:9)
- "If any man be in Christ, he is a new creature: old things are passed away; behold, all things are become new." (2 Corinthians 5:17)

Your Part:

- **Repent** (Turn from your sins)

"Except ye repent, ye shall all likewise perish." (Luke 13:3)

- **Believe**

"Believe on the Lord Jesus Christ, and thou shalt be saved, and thy house." (Acts 16:31)

- **Do It Now**

"Seek ye the Lord while he may be found, call ye upon him while he is near." (Isaiah 55:6)

"Behold, now is the day of salvation." (2 Corinthians 6:2) "How shall we escape, if we neglect so great salvation?" (Hebrews 2:3)

- **Remember**

"Every one of us shall give account of himself to God." (Romans 14:12)

"It is appointed unto men once to die, but after this the judgment." (Hebrews 9 : 27)

"But he that believeth on him...shall not come into judgment." (John 5:24)

"Choose you this day whom ye will serve." (Joshua 24:15)

Are you ready to believe right now? If so, simply tell God what he asked you to confess. You might use a prayer similar to this one:

"God, I admit to you that I am a sinner and I know I cannot do anything to earn my way to Heaven. I truly believe that Jesus died on the cross, was buried and rose from the grave. I put my faith in His sacrifice to pay for my sin in full."

FAMILY OF GOD FELLOWSHIP

1471 Pine Road
(PO Box 831313)
Ocala, FL 34483-1313
jamessnyder2@att.net
www.whatafellowship.com
www.jamessnyderministries.com

SUNDAY

10:30AM	Worship Celebration Children's Church
5:30 PM	Adult Bible Study WOL Clubs

WEDNESDAY

6:30 PM	Family Focus Night WOL Clubs

For confidential prayer & counseling

**Please call Pastor Snyder at
1-352- 687-4240**

FAMILY OF GOD FELLOWSHIP
exists to GLORIFY God and CELEBRATE the Christian experience through Fellowship, Discipleship and Stewardship

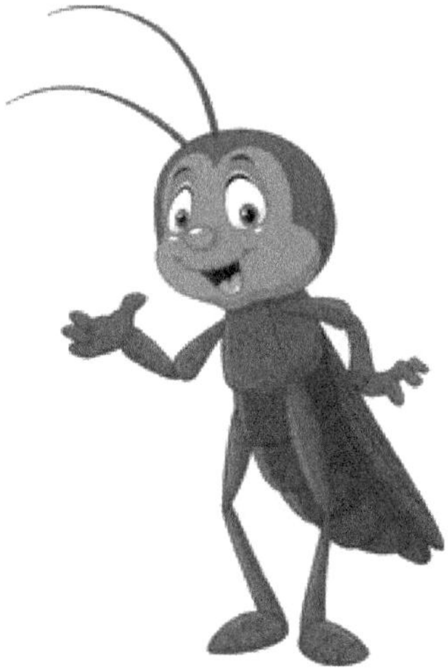